HEAVEN OF THE MOMENT

HEAVEN OF THE MOMENT

POEMS BY JOHN C. MORRISON

Fairweather Books • Brownsville, Oregon

First Edition 2 3 4 5 6 7 8 9

Library of Congress Cataloging in Publication Data
John C. Morrison,
Heaven of the Moment
ISBN 13: 978-0-9771973-7-8
ISBN 10: 0-9771973-7-9
Library of Congress Control Number: 2007936704

Fairweather Books is an imprint of
Bedbug Press
P.O. Box 39
Brownsville, OR 97327
www.bedbugpress.com

Cover Art: *Uno y el Universo* by Francisco Souto
Author Photo: Kathryn Krygier
Design: Cheryl McLean

Printed by Thomson-Shore, Inc., Dexter, Michigan.

This book is printed on acid-free paper.

ACKNOWLEDGMENTS

My sincere appreciation goes to the editors at these publications in which the following poems first appeared, sometimes in earlier versions:

Caffeine Destiny: "Bluegill Dawn," "Evidence at the Moon Winx Motel," "Ice Lament," and "Moon at Shuffleboard"
California Quarterly: "Two Sides of Dusk"
Cimarron Review: "My Neighbor's Dog" and "The Night Before Coyotes"
Comstock Review: "Spinoza and the Morning"
Good Foot: "Black Bead" and "The Former Beauty Queen of Livingston, Montana"
Hubbub: "Mass," "The Scour," and "Spider Weather"
Manzanita Quarterly Literary Review: "A Hundred Years Ago" and "Porch Steps"
Natural Bridge: "How the Rain Leaves"
Oregon Literary Review: "Heaven of the Moment" and "My Memory Begins with the Grass"
Poetry East: "The Eighth Hole with My Father"
Poet Lore: "Notes Between Swing and Graveyard"
The Oregonian: "Promise of More"
Seattle Review: "Pearl of Bone"
Southern Poetry Review: "Cajun C" and "Pine Siskin"
Sycamore Review: "My Son the Houdini"
Tar River Poetry: "Ma 'Cille's Museum of Miscellany"
Windfall: "New Patch of Sky"

"A Hundred Years Ago" was also nominated for a Pushcart Prize.

My sincere appreciation to Literary Arts, Inc., and their patrons for an Oregon Literary Fellowship that brought much of this collection together, and to Caldera for a residency that provided a balance of quiet and camaraderie.

Many fine poets and dear friends were deeply generous in helping me shape, over time, these poems and this book, especially my teachers Gary Thompson, Debora Greger, Dara Wier, Tom Rabbitt, and Peter Sears; gifted readers Paulann Petersen, Judith Montgomery, Jess Lamb, Garth Weber, Dave Jarecki, and Maureen MacAvoy Jemison; the Odd Monday poets who have shared many warm evenings with me over the years; and my kind publisher, Tony Gorsline, and the fine folks at Bedbug Press. My gratitude also to my family, my sons, and to Kim Thomas, who offered only unwavering encouragement.

Contents

I. Porch Steps

II. Pine Siskin

III. PROMISE OF MORE

Date your letters in detail like this.
We're living in such a world
that the month, the day, the hour
contain more writing than the thickest book.

Nazim Hikmet, "Hello Everybody"

for

Jon Hershey

I. Porch Steps

PORCH STEPS

The sun, like a tall yellow house, rises
on the block where I park for work.
A woman in white pajamas
sits on the front steps and drinks coffee
from a dark mug. We always smile
and wave as I walk to a job

I forget as it happens, as though
penciled notes fade each time
I turn the page. And she?
If I didn't have my own life,
I'd invite myself up for a cup
and conversation, risk lifting

into the spring sky just to see
from that vantage the day
take shape. Settled in a spare room,
I'd pitch in around the cosmos to earn
my keep: bolt gravity tight
at the poles and equator

of new planets, bend light around
black holes, and give directions
to the recent dead: After two days,
you'll reach heaven. Saints take
a day to review your soul,
sins, misgivings. That's all I know.

Notes Between Swing and Graveyard

We were on our first real wage job, summer
at the Del Monte plant,
at night an island of pink light
in the wide valley's dark sea.
After a month of apricot, we
sorted tomatoes from rats for ketchup,
soup, sauce, and saved the firm
for Safeway. The married few
on the shift made each of us long
for a lover to make money beside us

and then, at home in an apartment
on Iowa or Mays Street, wander her body
still damp from sweat, still dulled
by work into the morning, as far
as muscle could last. Without a wife,
without a girlfriend, and so worn out
by the season of packing and canning
that took us with sore hands and sour hair
to the lip of sunrise, who would have us?

Who could find us? We began to swap notes
with the senoritas and girls
from the other high school who giggled
and left swing as we pulled up for graveyard.
More florid each night, more freighted
with moon and stars and promises,
our missives were drawn on jagged corners
of kraft paper used to line the crates
of ripening fruit. I wrote to Reneé,

and she wrote back and we never said
a word on the thick folds slipped
in each other's locker. I'd write at break, the dead
center of night, as her strawberry hair
must've spilled across her pillow in sleep.
Her notes to me I would jam unread into my
jeans pocket rather than ever share
with my friends. Shift's end, in the gravel
parking lot, before starting my ailing truck

and heading off, slowly I'd unfold
her sweet cursive like the gift it was,
as the light outlined the distant Sierra,
with day just coming up around me
and read and know her teases
counted like a dream left in sleep.

NIGHT DOG

Fat tumors at spine, at
belly, growths like burrs at eyelids,
lips, our old dog on rickety
back legs hauls up his
bulk from beside our bed,
dodders around the night house.

Darkness doesn't matter in the dim.
He finds his way by the shape
scents take inside the house and out
where he can sniff for an hour
shrubs, tree trunks, the stiff
crap of other dogs, and wag.
Even winter blossoms.

He wobbles through the rooms
like any elder too bored or sore
to sleep, finds the kitchen bowl,
crunches a bite of kibble, laps
a tongue or two of water, comes back
to our floor, eases down with a grunt,
and sighs. In the day we humans

have become miraculous. Appear
from nowhere beside him, muzzle
buried to his eyes in vinca.
He startles as I stroke ghostly fur
on top of his head and when
time's up, I'll hook a finger under
his collar, lead him to the door.

BLACK BEAD

Hunched like a grey bear over
my ten-year-old hand, my father spun
in his knobby fingers a drill bit
thin as a toothpick on my bruised thumbnail.

In the solitary game where I slammed
grey rock against grey rock, the rock
all our dry acre had in abundance,
I missed on my way to open the color

inside: sunrise, ochre, rust, willow green.
Under my thumb's clear, fine shell
a thundercloud appeared in the pink sky,
a cloud that brooded, brooded but wouldn't

rain, only throbbed darker. He never
offered what he knew, not the science
of winds, not constellations, not the curve
of the earth, but he would go quiet, lean in,

and try to fix anything. Clumsy about gentleness,
silver flashed in his hand. He whispered,
How brave you are, as he churned, then coaxed
out the pinhole a first bead of black blood.

YOUNG BUCK

With my late teens a wait for any seduction,
my summer boss, CQ, said, *Stay.* He meant
a union card, union wage, a chance to drive
the Cat and learn the recipe and ratios of sand,
water, aggregate, and cement for concrete.

I'd have been right behind Michael, stocky,
blond, and still drunk from his twenty-first birthday,
on work's stepladder. He'd drive up in a new blue
four-by-four pickup, as far off the ground
as the world of men, climb down as his wife,
Danielle, a slender plume of amber smoke,
slid over, took the wheel and rolled away

to return at lunch to sit beside him
in the high cab and pull their sandwiches
and soda from a cooler. I weighed out
what that sweet life was worth as I shoveled
and hauled gravel from one pile to another.
A sure job or school in the foothills
where I could flirt with women
who perfumed with patchouli.

I handed CQ my hard hat, scuffed
but still bright orange as the hazy sun
that rose across the river, rose
over my shoulder as I arrived at work,
the hard hat that sat on my head
like another head, with another brain
on top a body a bit more tan
and brawny, with calloused hands and booted feet
and a mind that wanted to say, *I'll stay.*

ICE LAMENT

My first day at Queen City Ice
was my last, leather-gloved
in the freezer hefting ice blocks
for the wiry, cold-eyed foreman whose
white office wall held the state portrait
of George Wallace, smiling,
flanked by the American flag.
He chased me from the blue
saying, *Gid out*, as though his ice,
frozen right out of the tap,
right out of the amber water
of Lake Tuscaloosa, was too pure
for all of God's children. In
the crystalline air, his nose keen
as a hound dog's, he claimed to scent
sour beer from the night before, *so gid out*.

We weren't about to get along.
His family was ice, and I
only wanted summer work
out of the humid, hellish season,
to walk to my job under the dark limbs
of live oak, to labor cold and dry, to feed
the chute silvery blocks to grind
coarse or fine, to dump for a fisherman,
his pickup backed up to the dock,
a half barrel of cubes into the cooler
of catfish stink-bait, warm, rotted cheese,
a half barrel of crushed
into his cooler of sandwiches
and beer, and to walk home,
still chill, across the tracks
as the late afternoon thunderstorms
broke up and the asphalt street steamed.

My Accent

Not a music nor motion of tongue
and lips I was born to, more a lilt
learned leaning close to Blue's stories
of barnstorm baseball as we ripped
out, at an hourly wage, the kudzu vines
that choked the state park in Moundville,
taking care to step around sleepy

terrapins, or maybe as I had lunch
in the voices at the crowded City Café,
a short ride over the Black Warrior River,
my plate piled with pulled pork, fried okra,
corn muffins, and black-eyed peas.
Roy Orbison's vibrato on the jukebox,
the talk around the tables all feed stores
and first wives. In the hazy town,

a car parts store manager could mistake me
for a guy working at the tire factory,
married to a thin, nervous, smarter woman
who yearns to have a baby, a town where
the iced tea is always sweet, beer
always cheap, and where when a friend
said, *Hey*, she meant, *Hello,*
how are you, and *Don't let me keep you.*

THE SCOUR

No kiss or sandwich could stall her
as she scoured and cursed the woman
who last lived in her new apartment,
who left a greasy kitchen sink that reeked,

a dumped ashtray under couch cushion,
and thriving amber cockroaches
inside the kitchen wall. A woman,
I told her, I knew, though never well.

Angeline, her eyes were a quick, hard blue.
She'd say words like *luminous, chintzy*
and *moon*. Stopping with her on the grey
sidewalk outside the High Hat, a run-

down lounge, I stood like rookie spelunker
at the mouth of a gem cave where rose crystals
bloomed in the dark and, odds were, once in
I'd never return. The woman I would marry

jerked back a dusty drape to swear and stand
in the sunlit breeze. Within minutes I was on knee
to scrub tub and around toilet, floors
and door jamb with cleansers that left

my hands raw, as though I'd clambered up
a rock face. Pink, they tingled all night.

Ma 'Cille's Museum of Miscellany

Nothing's funny about amateur taxidermy
gone awry. Ma practiced on whatever animal,
farm or wild, slaughtered or rifle-shot, the day
delivered dead to the shed door of her
Island of Dr. Moreau. She began simple, planted

deer antlers into jackalope brow,
and progressed over years to turtledove
housed in terrapin shell; perfect coonhound,
the bandit's head tacked to a blue tick; mer-
woodchuck with lacquered tail of large-mouth bass.

But she never conquered her craft. A strip
of hide lolls from a dairy cow's flank
like a tongue. The panther's sunken marble eye
stares at constellations etched on the inside
of the skull. Stitches give and spill

cotton fill. And genius she was, she lost passion
halfway through the last incarnation.
In the rainbow light of a window lined
with her antique tonic bottles, the hog-swan
trumpets, reaches for flight with one wing.

BLUE HANDS

My son at eighteen months
squeezed the ink pad so long
his hands moved through blue
to black, night sky without moon
or clouds or stars: indigo.

How was he not frightened
by those hands? The ink set
layers deep, stained, I thought,
to the skin he would wear
for his second birthday. He repeated,

Blue hands, while we sat
in the tub scrubbing for forty minutes
with mechanic's soap
and a coarse rag. *Blue hands*.
Cobalt, then Prussian.

Next morning another bath
with a rag and blue hands,
royal blue. The dye began to lift,
night letting go, giving to day,
azure, finally, robin's egg.

The last trace left that afternoon
as he played beside me in the flower bed.
I planted bulbs. He sifted
for pebbles then lifted from the soil
the pink morning of his hands.

NEW PATCH OF SKY

Crows caw confused, the air
out of place. Light stands
stunned inside the drip line
that belonged to the spruce.

Blue from trunk to tip,
it crowded sewer pipe, scraped
eaves in every jagged wind.
I gave it a year to stunt,

stall at chimney height
and when in spring it flaunted
a fresh swarm of swollen,
soft buds, I hired Fred

in torn and stained pink jeans
to chainsaw and haul all
even memory away
with the squirrel nest tucked

in the branches: knotted ball
of duff and bark strands,
rotted strips of red rag
and green jute twine.

Home from school my youngest,
silent at the stump,
hands deep-rooted in pockets,
counts rings back to blur

around his birthday.
I knew he'd side with the spruce,
be too angry to see
the new patch of sky.

A HUNDRED YEARS AGO

1

The oncologist tells me, *You'd be dead,*
his one eye grim, the other, well, grim.
A hundred years ago, I tie
holster laces tight around my thigh,
kiss my wife—a hardworkin',
handsome woman, her hair swept up
in a blue kerchief—say, *Shoot, gal,*
doncha worry, t'aint nuthin',

while inside I fret, hope my swollen,
lumpy huevo is right tomorrow,
lean and ride the high meadow
to mend fence. Clouds skirt the summer sky
and I tire. Come winter, I can't leave
bed, a stiff ache like cold lead
along my spine, a wheezing cough
brings up nothing.

2

Still, with celestial timing, I fathered
my second child who squirmed into conception
in my last weeks of healthy sperm
but would've been gone by his birth, his slow
turn out of the womb, fresh
from the core of the universe and pissed
at the interruption of his
so peaceful sailing.
                    That explains why
when my son's ice-sharp eyes saw me
haloed, I'm sure, by the hospital lights,
he knit his scuffed brow to wonder,

                    What are you doing here?

3

Call the timing of my life
luck, luck to be not yet ghosted
by disease or calamity. Luck to be
nine years into the snores
of my summer child, sleeping deep
until late, nine years into waking

beside my wife to the slow tick
of rain, into days of slow work
however dull, evenings at home
however slow. Luck to carry
at the base of my sternum
a drear, blue star used to aim
the heavy radiation beam
gunning for my belly's lymph nodes
and any loose seeds of cancer.
Luck to be here just to say, *Boo.*

MY SON THE HOUDINI

After breakfast I chain
his wrists, ankles, lift
and lay him in a casket, kiss
his forehead, padlock and plunge
the heavy box into the icy river.

A minute later, I panic
peel away shoes to dive in
and he rises soaked, shivering
and beaming on the rocky shore
of the far bank. Then he's over

the rise to school where bored
in class he folds in half,
again in half, folds, folds,
with smart creases, folds
until he lies on the desktop
like a well-worn wallet

his teacher, Mr. Jaybird,
opens to find three dollars
for lunch, a matinee
movie stub, and a photo:

my boy grins, gives the camera
a wave, behind him
hand on his shoulder
all smiles, me, his old man.

EVENING DRESS

for my son

One day the sky will open,
promise, like there's a zipper
invisible from our side. One

long zip from zenith,
where cirrus clouds curve
mare tail strands, down

to the horizon, green peaks
of distant spruce trees. What's next?
What's behind? No, it's not

a giant pant fly, God's prick
ready to douse our world, his infinite
love and patience at end. No.

Promise. The sleek zipper
belongs to the back of a long
dress. From sweet wisps at cool nape

down to dimple a tip of the tongue
above the buttocks. While everyone
goes about their day in cars,

on sidewalks, in dusty offices,
all beholden to a dull script,
you will see what to reach for

as the dress slips off into evening,
into darkness. Promise. Close your eyes,
draw her close, breathe stars.

II. PINE SISKIN

SPIDER WEATHER

These are the warm calm
days before fall strips the trees
and rain turns the ground slick
the sky unpredictable,

the days of yellowjackets and fruit flies
that hover over the last wave of fallen
apples and grapes. I'm spending time
with the fat orange and brown spiders
tying pitchfork handle to compost bin,
house to camellia, camellia to spruce,
spruce to the blooming red dahlia.

Though almost brittle to touch,
the webs flex with the breeze, suspended
by strands taller than the kitchen windows.
If one ruptures, if a trapped moth tears
free, the scent in the air

says there is still time to mend
to thrive even as the flies are fewer
with the season's change before the first storm
shreds then washes the weaving away.

HOW THE RAIN LEAVES

Of course, everywhere someone is dying
or already dead. Inside, cakes, cheeses,

salads, and utensils crowd the table,
while our cousin's family and friends

begin the story on a different day
perhaps in a different town. Each one

ends at the moment when they'd heard
his heart quit beating

in Bellingham, overlooking the cold blue waters
and islands of the far Northwest.

On the gently sloping street in front,
my ten-year-old and I throw the baseball.

Horsehide slaps into the pocket, then
a little echo, like a curious afterthought,

from the facing houses. Slap, throw,
slap, throw, and alone we watch

the sun burn off the last overcast
as rain leaves the surrounding roofs

and the asphalt at our feet in long peels of steam
until we stand in the clouds.

MOON AT SHUFFLEBOARD

The moon, so often busy plying
the night sky, steps into the corner pub.
We end up playing shuffleboard on the long,
blond grain of a table milled from pine.

Everyone else sips warm beer
in the smoky air. Young, I practiced
the life of a Chinese poet, entirely
in translation, and lay a little drunk

in the tall grass of an abandoned olive grove
to watch the hillcrest glow and grow sharper
with backlight, sharper, then the crickets hushed
and she rose, just a wisp of cloud beneath

like sea foam. To see her step into
the olive branches strained my throat, her farther
away glancing through the limbs. I slept,
woke cold. Soon as I stumbled from the orchard

the moon and I grew more comfortable
with each other. She watches for me,
I think. At shuffleboard, her luminous touch
is soft. My game is no challenge for her.

I squint, aim, give a gentle push, and my puck
flies from the table to gutter. She smiles,
takes her turn in a whisper. You'd never guess
she pulls tides in the back of her mind.

The Night Before Coyotes

The night before coyotes
got my chickens, my neighbor
Karen and I were driving back
from the movies, and her horse
Glory Dell broke through my headlights
in an instant where my heart
fumbled for explanation, then paused,
and I thought, *Oh, that's it,*
I must be awake in a dream.
We pulled off to the side of Gordon Road
and walked under the heavy moon
toward the pasture where Glory
bowed to graze. We led her home,
our arms sometimes linked. Though
somewhere in the valley—at one
of the lights we could see from the hump
in the road—men and women tired
of the week must have been drinking beer,
hollering, and fighting, for us
the night seemed peaceful and we,
alone. We crossed my back property
on the way to Karen's barn and saw

the chickens asleep, roosting, their heads
tucked under their wings. She looped
Glory's rein around a low oak limb
and we dropped to moist grass,
finding our way past buttons, buckles,
and underwear, leaning into
an hour-long kiss. I believe the coyotes
came that night for the chickens
and discovered us wrapped
in what we thought was our solitude:
the lead animal nodding his wet jowls
in frustration as I appeared meaty
but bloodless rising and falling
washed in the moonlight.

BLUEGILL DAWN

In the morning oak, redwings trill
and chatter. Bluegill and bass pluck

struggling insects off the face of the lake,
leave silent, widening circles.

The big fish rests his belly on mud
in the shallow water. Hathaway aches

to slip a barbed hook through the muscle
of its lower jaw. Ball cap low, tongue

pink between his lips, he's all in one
concentration, fly-casting with a popper,

a cast each step. Across the water
he glides around a bend as I pause

to take bluegill from the weeds
along the bank and see dawn

in the subtle scales down their sides:
dark blue for the early sky,

green for the line of hills, rose
for the clouds, white, first light.

A THANK-YOU

Every morning
the world
is created.
        Mary Oliver

Yes. But by whom?
Who created our children
sleeping, Will snoring
through his nose?

Who stole the whole house,
as darkness came on,
ripping it out by the basement,
leaving a hole with

sewer and water and electrical
going nowhere as the moon
lolled through the sky,
only to create it again

in the dim light of dawn,
the foundation complete,
plumbing, flawless. Who put
us back, put Kim beside me,

our one thigh the tie
between these twins? Who
touched her? Who
lifted me, hands around

my cold ribs and shook out
all the hate and pity I collected
the day before? Who let me
start over one more time?

A Stake for the Red Dahlia

The resonance that rolled from sledge
up my arm to shoulder must've rung
in the ground nest like the pounding
of war. Yellowjackets, bees that see us
as meat, swirled as I scanned the sky for signs
of weather and were at once up pant legs,
tucked in armpit, latched on plump earlobe.
I swelled like a pudgy baby, and the doctor
leaned over me, slid the needle into my arm
and said the next sting could kill me.

Months later my neighbor and I followed one
to dozens whirring in and out
an old gopher den. We came back at night,
shined the flashlight on sleeping wings,
on armor with exact, cold markings
of yellow and black. We poured in
a jar of white gas, threw the lit match
for our barefoot toddlers, for dogs
dozing at the water bowl. The hole flickered,

sizzled, went silent. Another hive will rise
to repay me. First startled, I'll swat, yelp,
and dash a vain, spastic dash out to clear field and sky
where my capillaries will pop and tingle,
nerves jig down my neck, trunk, limbs, as I dance
and spin the last moment in the wind
of an exhilarated mind.

Two Sides of Dusk

Geese, they have an answer
for everything: wind, slugs, marriage,
aging. We walk back from the ballfield,
my twelve-year-old and I. His pitches
begin to travel along sinew from base of toes
to snap of wrist, to sing, if you have the ear.

He learns, gracefully, to be done with me
for now. Anymore, my curveball won't wobble
or even tilt, nothing like how
our earth quietly turns a season.

We stop to hear the hidden flock honk,
comical, insistent, above the low clouds
that hasten our dusk. They call in flight
across a sky where they see the fading sun
light a fiery ocean stretching to darkness.

PINE SISKIN

A name that won't quite rhyme
with *wise citizen*. Drunk on
pyracantha, small, crimson
berries with yellow dumpling inside,
the siskin mistook the reflection of lush
sweetgum for safe perch. A *whump*
jerked me from coffee, my son
from toast. Who wouldn't need
a minute to clear his head?
He lay stunned still, dusky
brown with yellow wing bars.
We prepared a warm towel,
an open shoe box on the lawn.
In an hour, revived, he was gone.

A dozen different birds,
robins, tanagers, sparrows, wrens,
have died in my clumsy care,
suffocated on worm segments,
drowned by forced water drops.
I've tried to learn. At thirteen,
I was the siskin. In play,
a sharp elbow to the chin and I
forgot everything for a time.
Lay quiet in the dust, while my
antsy, frightened friends ringed me.
Dirty faced, down at their upper lips
beaded with grey sweat, breath heaving
from the game—they should've
terrified me. The moment I didn't know
anything, I knew my kind.

RATTLESNAKE

◆

Even after the head's hacked off
the heart won't quit until sundown.

◆

Gutting, we discover halfway down
the slit in the tough, white belly

the small, pink silk purse,
mechanical, persistent.

◆

A yellowjacket that scents
the bloody discards, feeds

on the sac behind the fang–
poison still potent–

his sting could cripple a dog,
kill a child.

◆

Unless you're a mouse or toad
a rattler wants to be left alone, doze

on a warm rock, ease
prey down the tunnel of ribs.

◆

We sauté the skinned, pale
rope, spice the meat

with too much pepper and paprika,
burn our mouths on the mistake.

Evidence at the Moon Winx Motel

The Moon Winx winked at me once.
My friend Hershey and I were staying
a couple nights to visit and see
how the years had moved on without us.
To get lost then leave for good,
shake the dust from our boots, spit
in the Black Warrior River and go.

The garish, neon sliver of a moon,
floating outside our window beside the ragged
highway, didn't help. What did we want
but to live our lives forgiven and free
of earlier blunders and the moon
against the night sizzled from wide eye
to *wink*, wide eye to *wink*, wide eye to *wink*.

The bathroom wall is what I can't forget.
The second night I woke, heard the train
in the darkness, miles off in the sparse
pine woods, heard the slow coal barges
on the river, got up to piss and stared
at the wall past the mirror to see
a batch of botched plaster, the spread
of a shotgun blast. Under the wink
of a moon who always knew what you
were up to, someone had had enough,

held the barrel to his temple
and pushed the trigger with a thumb.
I ran my fingers along someone's
sloppy mending, lumpy like salmon roe,
where the gore must've hung, buckshot
buried beneath, like touching a fossil,
not the life but time and the hollow left behind.

LIFE FLIGHT

Just once I want that outrageous racket
to come for me. Not if it means I'm near dead,
hips shattered, my pants shitty, my wife wracked
by dread. Maybe a persistent crick in my neck

and sure enough I'm off in a hamlet
on a forested mountain ridge, and the big, loud bug
drops over the peaks of the firs, the limbs
all waving and crazy, and the pilot
negotiates the facade of the dry goods store,
the one stoplight, to land square on Main.

And all the townspeople crowd around in the raucous wind
to see the new guy safely off, a thrilled pity
on their faces. I'm brave, boy, I'm brave,
and they strap me and my little gurney
next to the portal window, tubing and wires
going everywhere, and *whoosh* we're in the air
and noise, in the constant clatter as we sail
over ravines and rivers, bound for the city.

The poor bastard ferried overhead to Emanuel
may be a goner. His last sight the flash
of the running light reflected in the fog,
a rhythm to carry on without him.
The beep on the monitor flutters, pauses, stops,
and the EMT straddles and pumps his chest
and goes sore before the chopper touches down
on the roof pad where a doctor swears,
sighs, and calls the time of death, unless

we can imagine the run might be for me
or some other game schmuck who plays the role
to keep the crew sharp. Life Flight whisked
to the woods on a lark, while on the wet streets
below we can look up to the buzz, cheer,
and say, *Lucky dog, they're making great time.*

THE EIGHTH HOLE WITH MY FATHER

Persephone, the tormented goddess
trapped in hell at the birth
of the Christian era, walks alone
in the caverns of the tortured dead,
and Lucifer, hidden in a cleft
of rock, finds her. She does not
relent. He kicks, gouges her back
with his split hooves; *Damn,*
Dad says, *The Devil's beating*
his wife again, and it rains
while the sun shines on pastures,
farmland, and the eighth hole
across the river from Canby.

We pick up our bags, kick sod
from our cleats, step out from under
the gazebo raised in honor
of a deceased golfer, as the rain
becomes a spit, leaves droplets
like sequins on the shoulder
and sleeves of our sweaters.
He tees, stretches his back,
his driver held out like a cane.
I'm gonna get ahold of this one,
I'm gonna get ahold of this one.
He steps up with the wood
that weighs heavier with each swing.

There is an obscuring rise
on this hole, a ridge
where the pines step down a soft slope
to the green. You have to square
your ball with where you remember
the pin to be: between the pond,
murky, swimming with bluegill,
and the ravine of briar and nettles,
hold the pin in mind,
the damp flag limp on the breeze.

When the stroke is perfect,
the club face open to meet the ball
at the point of upswing, the ball leaves the tee
in a whisper, and there's time
for me to stand beside my father
as the sprinkle begins again:
Persephone's cool tears on the back
of our hands while we shade
our eyes, watch the ball lift
into a crease of sunlight.

When we believe the ball has reached
its height, egg-shaped as it is on impact,
the elastic wound round the center
releases, and spherical,
the ball climbs a minute more,
for us a minute longer,
before dropping over the crest,
bound for the imagined green.

MY MEMORY BEGINS WITH THE GRASS

No sleep could be sweeter
than the icy night I nestled
in a strip of brittle grass,
the sky too cold for snow.

My spinning was the spinning
of the galaxy, and who
could say otherwise
as my blood darkened, thickened

like pitch? The cop knelt,
his huge mitt on the loose zipper
of my cloth coat. My ghost,
the sober, sour half of me,

already risen, all ready to be
wind and shadow, leaned to his ear,
whispered, *Let the boy go.*
See how peaceful he is?

The cop looked up to the frozen
indifferent clouds, down
to my sodden blue face, paused
then gave me one good shake.

HEAVEN OF THE MOMENT

Our love would be enough as long as we
never left the county by the highway north
to Montgomery and across the bridge arched
over the muddy Tombigbee. She
feared falling, how the high arc might buckle
like flimsy tin and our car tumble
to the alligator roil in the swamp below.

My problem was the sky. The span aimed us
to whatever weather was there: plump,
lazy thunderheads, hazy sunshine, heavy rain,
or night and stars that seethed as we
came closer. Gravity could forget to keep
our tires tight to the road and the ramp
would fling us into the heaven of the moment
where she and I were sure to let go.

III. Promise of More

PEARL OF BONE

Leaning out from the rocky mountainside,
Jerome, Arizona, waits for the secret
uranium mine beneath the streets
to open the next unsteady spar,
to crack wide a crevice and slide.
Whole blocks of delicate blown glass,
antique shops, and churches, in spite of faith,

will follow the collapsed jail fourteen miles
to the washed-out floor of the Verde Valley.
The cloud could linger for days. I question
our waitress. Isn't she afraid some night
after too many beers she'll slip off the curb
and roll and roll and roll until all

that reaches the river is a polished pearl
of bone? No. Born here, she's once
been as far as Prescott, claims she'd walk tilted,
then topple on flat land. The same grim slope
where gravity waits to betray me,
she balances the angle and serves my family.

The Serial Hat

At twelve, my grandfather gone,
no one kept me from late
TV. In reruns of grey serials

from just before the war,
the Rocketman wore a golden
bullet helmet, thin slits for

eyes and mouth. Steely-stoic,
he'd descend, revolver drawn,
on a clutch of thieves. Wisecracks

echoed from behind the blank face.
In his secret identity, his
walking-around life, his lunch-

at-the-counter, gin-after-work life,
the two-bit gumshoe
dressed in a dull suit with a hat

the twin of my grandfather's.
His clients stiffed him. His girl
pouted. One grim episode, in his civvies,

without helmet, heater, leather jacket,
or jet pack, he took a pratfall
into a den of Nazis. Fists flew.

Chairs shattered. Lips bled.
Punches landed like raps on a coffin lid.
The Rocketman crashed three, four

times to the floor. Roped to a post
he slumped, limp, pale
as a raw shrimp peeled from shell.

But the hat, through the scuffle,
stayed snug on his head
like my grandfather's

dimpled grey fedora in his last weeks
on the walk with cane to Mass,
rakish on defiant brow.

THE FORMER BEAUTY QUEEN
OF LIVINGSTON, MONTANA

A storm of soft, grey insects overwhelmed
the wipers, smeared in the last wash spray.
Dad drove the station wagon
with one eye out the open window
into the next town. At a lit Texaco,
he hosed away the windshield goo,
refilled the cleaning fluid. Standing
outside the car, he leaned to Mom's ear,
said we should stay the night, let
the bugs above the rice fields settle
in the morning sun and fresh breeze.
Sick of sitting, sick of Cheez-Its,

we were all for a cheap motel with TV,
cots, and itchy blankets. Mom said no.
She was set on getting home and would
rather stare awake every dark hour
than step onto an orange shag carpet,
lips tense, and scan the dingy
wall paint, bland landscape prints, and green
plaid bedspread. I know now her youth

was gone and what she had to show
was her man in a thin tee shirt and a car
full of six kids who knew when to shut up.
We rolled back onto the highway
sulky, anxious about the looming
rice fly barrier, to save her from turning sleepless
against the rough sheets of a stale room.

MASS

The church of the Holy Ghost
is God's long shoe box, pale
wood and windows stained with angels
or mute saints. Stephen, arrows
hanging from his trunk, groin,
and thighs, looks skyward.

In the opening hymn, my father's voice,
so low and lazy on the register,
never finds the note. I despise
my raw chin and blocky brown
hand-me-down shoes that won't fit.

I have to pee but I don't squirm,
because Jesus is here and there's proof.
The lit gold lamp suspended
over the altar tells us
the Eucharist is consecrated
and God is in his house.

I stare above my folded hands.
How does the flame ignite?
By itself? At the right instant?
What is a prophet, as in,
He testified through the prophets?
A bulbous microphone like one
at the Sermon on the Mount,
one like Jesus might lean into
for testimony before the Romans
or Pharisees? I kneel and gnaw
on the soft, dark, salty top
of the pew like a porcupine.

PRICK

With Dad away in a war story,
Mom asked Mose, my drunk
uncle, to give me the talk.
At eleven, I already know
the three ways to start a baby.

Deep tongue kissing, seeds like tadpoles
swim the saliva from man's mouth
to woman's and race to her belly.
The winner sticks like a budding oak ball
outside the soft sack of the bladder.
That's why pregnant women
pee all the time.

Or you could cram your wiener
into a girl's butthole, which is boring
'cause you have to lie there
until you pee, or something.

Last, the Genghis Khan method
can only work twice:
slice open your bag,
slip out one of your nuts
like a slimy eye, and you,
or in Khan's case a slave,
slide the warm globe of goo
up the woman's pee hole.

Mose tells me all wrong.
Walks me down to the shade
along the creek, holds his fist
at his pants fly and says,
A man gets all heated up
and then gets a prick, see?
and pops out his index finger.

Prick? Prick? Prick means needle
and blood to me. In what I know now
to be the timeless fuck gesture
he jams Mr. Pointer
through the tight loop
of index and thumb of the left hand,
And he sticks it in her cunt.

I couldn't figure him out;
the man spit and stumbled.
You got it now, okay?
He was thirsty
for a frosty beer and I'm sure
at home he told Mom, *Margaret,*
don't worry, the boy's taken care of.

POMEGRANATES

The farmer who could've blasted birdshot
to chase two stray boys home

ignored us. His tractor rumbled tilling weeds
between the long orchard rows of pear.

We dropped our bikes in a racket. Crows
cawed and scattered. We stood hushed

by what seemed spilled bushels
of pomegranates, rosy rinds split open

to garnets. I knew the myth where Persephone,
daughter of the grain goddess, a girl

gathering flowers, is caught by the waist
in the crook of Hades' arm

as his chariot pours into a gash in the earth
like oily water. For her each seed,

lit inside with ruby light
meant a month in the underworld. Autumn,

in the low sun, we picked through pith
and tossed the bitter and sweet

to our bellies, then left in the quiet,
smoky dusk, our hands stained dark blossoms.

NIGHT AT THE MONTEZUMA SLOUGH

The fall I fretted over tardy pubic hair,
my brother took me miles out
on gravel roads. Grey dust churned behind us.
We found the couch he'd hauled
from the dump, drunk, with friends in the first heat
of summer, settled to wood frame in salt grass
and muck. The dark stretched past
the few lights of Martinez on the far shore.

Rods weighted and rigged for stripers,
baited with half-frozen chunks of anchovy,
we wanted the rare sturgeon in from
the Pacific, long, muscular as a man's arm,
with spines that could slice open the palm.
Then, in the chill wait, a little tug,
a puny catfish, a closer cousin, Mike told me,
ugly as fact, with skin not scales and simple
lungs for taking air. An animal
almost ready to squirm onto land with us.

Why would I hold on? Up from the split cushion
of the rotting couch, up from sour beer
and the radio with country music
from Sacramento, I stood at the bank
of brackish slough in hand-me-down jacket
for gusts that stung the cheek, worked
the hook from sturdy jaw and slipped him back
into the water. We stayed on for nothing
until the cold outweighed the folly
of another cast, and drove out quiet, numb,
pointed to the weak glow above the line
of low hills, the one sign of town
in a landscape without landmark.

SAINT PATTY MARQUEZ

We feared the moment we'd become queer
in a blink the way bread became flesh, wine
blood, and that blink meant everything:
cussed at in the green tiled echo
of a crowded boys' bathroom, bones
brittle on the news, crotch left naked
and voice reedy forever. Only the reviled
would take you in. Mama's boys, the spastics,
the grubby, and God would lick your ass

with eternal flame. What would be
the cause for me? My dick painfully hard
beside my best friend's husky sleep breathing?
A drunk in the park unzipping tattered pants
to drag out his grey cock like a length
of cropped hose? A big girl in overalls
shoving me down the playground, grey
pea gravel embedded bloody in my palm,
my tears sticky as corn syrup?

My secret serum against the bug that waited
in the air or, already ingested, lay dormant
was to moon over Patty Marquez.
I'd stare out the corner of my sight,
half-afraid my vision would freeze to the side
and still stare until my eyes
were sore in their sockets. Black curls
piled high and bouncy, irises mysterious
blue, skin enticing as cold milk.

Did she know? It was enough to sit
a row away, have her call me by name,
and to have seen what I was sure
was the angel white sheen of her panties
one Friday afternoon as she changed
in the back of her mother's car
out of parochial red plaid into pants
for Anna Manglona's sleepover.

Patty Marquez, who was taken from me
when she moved for fifth grade,
was such medicine in our inherited, cruel
ignorance. My mind can't age her beyond
ten years. She remains for me like a waxen
saint, a relic at rest on silk, lying hidden
in the altar of an old stone church.

SKY TO SAGE

The crack and boom jars me
from a desert vacation drive
with sleeping family to see
the same highway twenty years ago
rendered in the black and white
of lightning. In back

of a U-Haul, door rolled open
for air, in the scent of ozone
and warm, wet pavement, I squatted,
jostled, in the racket
of shifting furniture, appliances.
Headed to the South, I'd hitched a ride
with Cash, a skinny veteran
dying of Agent Orange, and his family.

When he stood shirtless after a shower,
the affliction ran along the inside
of his arms and blazed across his chest
like a fierce sunburn. Addled, foul-tempered,
he'd slap his daughter and scold his wife
in cafés and campgrounds across
the great basin and over the Divide.

They were moving to her mother's farm
in Oklahoma so he could open
an arcade in nearby Checotah.
For an afternoon, I helped heft
pinball machines, their panels of busty,
cartoon women, into the dusty
unlit pool hall, and I knew his dream
would be a bad dream or worse.

No children on the sidewalks,
where were the pockets to reach into
for the grubby quarter, let alone quarter
after quarter after quarter,
enough to feed Eloise
and eleven-year-old Sophie?
Most way to my next life, I gave her my copy
of *Bulfinch's Mythology*
and left by Greyhound from Muskogee.

Her, her mother and skeletal father,
I'd forgotten them, then the bolts
ripped sky to sage.
Bituminous clouds low
above the highway, virga showers
let slip a few, fat drops
that hit the asphalt, shine
like coins to pay for passage.

PROMISE OF MORE

Forever, I thought, the freezer
would store an ice block or more of smelt,
silvery and silver-eyed and solid
in half-gallon milk cartons. My parents

and aunts and uncles went smelting,
wading into the Sandy or Clackamas River
to dip the long nets into the flashing
school. A hundred is a good day.

And I say without regret, when the season
came where the brothers and sisters
let pass the radio news that smelt
were running and stayed home, old,

aluminum nets hung in the garage,
I never knew I'd miss the fish. Not
for the salty bite, not for the crunch
of the spine or cornmeal crust,

but because they were on our table
an impossible plenitude. And I'd been served
my own oily, steaming plate stacked
with smelt, with the promise of more

if I wanted, and more after that,
and the house was a smoky light,
as it rained the steady rain of a forest,
a rain falling softly on all our rivers.

CAJUN C

The revolver's wood grip
warmed to the hand as we howled
and ripped off rounds at cans
trembling on the dirt mound.
A lovely, seductive .38
he inherited in a soft blue cloth
after his cursed brother's car wreck.
I should've told him to melt it down.
Instead, for twenty years he kept
the gun in the glove box for his suicide.

Melançon, he carried
a cedilla, a sickle, on the bottom
of his Cajun *c*, a sickle
I was sure he could detach
for a bloody fight with his drunk
father's ghost, or for a harvest.
Perhaps on a drive to the bayou
and cypress of Louisiana
to clear his head, he'd pull over
and lend a hand to gleaners
at the field's rough fringe.

That's more who he was,
the one in flannel shirt, jeans,
and work boots, throwing open
car door to holler, *Hey, y'all,
let me help*. Unhooking
the tool from the undercarriage
of his name, he would wade
into the grain and swing.

MY NEIGHBOR'S DOG

Better for me had my neighbor died
before we began to drink out our nights
at a table stained with red wine:
his eyes, two tight circular syllogisms,
two eight balls rolled back black and white
into his head. The old philosopher
who named his dog Being. Capital *B*,
Being. His colleagues at every
university struggle with phantom
answers. Professor Tiedeman dismisses
them as alchemists and names Being,
discovers Being becoming, Being,
which wasn't and now is, Being
born in a litter of nine retrievers.

And the world, roundly, makes too much sense,
like looking in your rearview
after a long day at the end
of a long, straight street to see
slow traffic laid out behind you:
braided silver glinting wet
in the sunlight through clouds. You say
how wonderful to sit still beside
a black van pumping country rock
at an interminable stoplight
and then be here: woven in the bright braid,
and then be here. Being is like that,
halfway in my tipped garbage can
one minute; the next, shredding
in his bird-soft mouth my copy
of the daily *Oregonian*.

I'm home Sunday, ignoring my headache
from La Salles, ignoring the sticky smell
of Chianti in my sinuses, the smell
of Tiedeman's tedious chatter,
his illicit flurries while his wife,
sweet Janice, sits home warming her feet
under the belly of Being,

Being. Ignore it all because my son
shouldn't see his old man drunk
or marred by wine. Better for him to play
street football unencumbered while I rake leaves
and the leavings of Being, lean
against the sweetgum and watch his team
huddle for a second down call.
Read the lips of my son, the light receiver,
he's telling Tiedeman's boy Lewis,
that foul-mouthed shit, *Throw it to me
on a fly pattern.* Bent over at their hips,
the five study the line my son
draws on his dirty palm, a crisp line
up the gutter to the Hubners' driveway.
The quarterback Lewis, always the arbiter
of cruel mediocrity, says
loudly enough for Being to hear
and howl out back, *Fuck you. Everyone
goes short.* Listen to him, son. Listen
hard. Listen to Being scratch at the fence gate.

SPINOZA AND THE MORNING

The surgeon knotted sutures one step
too slow to seal the net of vessels
oozing around his heart. Mother

rocked, framed by a window
shining on the penultimate hour.
Stunned, stuck like the late night

was clear pitch, I watched the dark
for sign of morning. Young, at school
I'd write for philosophy and push up

from the kitchen chair to step outside,
breathe, and see the strange stars
spun to us from the other hemisphere

and return with less time to Spinoza,
the lens grinder who taught relentless trust.
By morning when I packed my papers

in my bag and started toward campus,
I was drunk on exhaustion and his axiom
that we are God thinking. So let God learn regret.

A few years later at work, the other janitor
and I scrubbed floors, toilets, grime inside
light fixtures so close to sunrise, he insisted

we have the light find us facing west
and the great Sacramento Valley.
The streets were empty as we drove, reckless,

balancing large paper cups of dark beer
through the dim. We outlived our folly.
Spinoza wouldn't survive the glass dust

that lacerated his lungs. Dad,
bloated by another four liters of saline,
another twenty pounds of pressure to give his heart

traction, ceased, and three of us, quiet
as dust in the room, struggled to remember
how day begins. Those years before

out of the car and up the rocky hill's dirt path,
my friend and I turned to see
already it was bright morning across the river

in the towns of Fruto and Chrome. We stood
in the shadow of the Sierra
watching the wall of light careen our way,

emblazing pools of distant rice fields
and the deep green of almond orchards.
Faster than thought, light swept toward us,

claiming creek and stones, onto us
and over us, a wind from heaven to warm
our backs, lay our shadows in the grass.

About the Author

John C. Morrison received the 2004 C. Hamilton Bailey Poetry Fellowship from Literary Arts. His poems have appeared in numerous journals, including the *Seattle Review*, the *Cimarron Review*, and *Southern Poetry Review*. He directs the Writers in the Schools program for Literary Arts in Portland, Oregon, and also teaches poetry at Washington State University, Vancouver. This is his first collection of poetry.

On the cover: *Uno y el Universo* by Francisco Souto

ABOUT THE ARTIST

Francisco Souto was born in Venezuela. He earned his BFA from the Herron School of Art and Design in 2000 and his MFA from Ohio State University in 2002. He has participated in a wide range of national and international exhibitions throughout the world, including the 6th Kochi International Triennial Exhibition of Prints in Japan, the 4th Novosibirsk International Biennial of Contemporary Graphic Art in Russia, the 5th British International Miniature Print Exhibition, the 12th International Print Biennial in Bulgaria, the Boston Printmakers 2003 North American Print Biennial, the Los Angeles Printmaking Society's 18th National Print Exhibition, and the 2004 edition of Colorprint USA in Texas. He has taught workshops and has been a visiting artist at institutions throughout the United States and abroad, including Anderson Ranch Arts Center in Colorado; Universidad de los Andes in Venezuela; American University in Cairo, Egypt; the Finnish Academy of Fine Arts in Helsinki; the University of Texas at Austin; Kansas State University; and Columbus College of Art and Design in Ohio. He has received many awards and grants, and his work is part of many important public and private collections. He is currently Assistant Professor of Art in the Department of Art and Art History at the University of Nebraska–Lincoln.

Souto's *Uno y el Universo* (One and the Universe), the cover print, is based on a book of the same title by the Argentine writer Ernesto Sábato. For Souto, the very personal universe, with all its flaws and contradictions, is the only path to finding yourself. The Roman numeral on the bottom of the print represents the date the print was finished: "ANNO IX MMIV" (September 2004).

ABOUT THE PUBLISHER

Bedbug Press was founded in 1995 by Tony Gorsline, who has had a lifelong love of books and writing. Under the imprints Cloudbank Books and Fairweather Books, Bedbug Press has published thirteen books of poetry, a creative nonfiction memoir, and a series of children's coloring books.

In 2003, the press established The Northwest Poetry Series with the publication of *My Problem with the Truth* by Chris Anderson. Since then three more books by Northwest poets have been added to the series: *Insects of South Corvallis* by Charles Goodrich, *Out of Town* by Lex Runciman, and *A Bride of Narrow Escape* by Paulann Petersen.

Also in 2003, the press began an annual poetry contest, The Rhea & Seymour Gorsline Poetry Competition. The contest offers a cash prize and publication of the winning manuscript. *Textbook Illustrations of the Human Body* by George Estreich (Corvallis, OR) was the winner of the 2003 contest. *Solar Prominence* by Kevin Craft (Seattle, WA) was the 2004 winner, and *Gathering Sound* by Susan Davis (Chapel Hill, NC) and *Friday and the Year That Followed* by Juan J. Morales (Pueblo, CO) were cowinners of the 2005 prize.

Bedbug Press authors have received a number of honors: Barbara Koons (*Night Highway*), first finalist for the 2006 Best Books of Indiana Awards; David Hassler (*Red Kimono, Yellow Barn*), 2006 Ohio Poet of the Year; Paulann Petersen (*A Bride of Narrow Escape*), recipient of the Stewart H. Holbrook Literary Legacy Award and a finalist for the 2006 Oregon Literary Arts Oregon Book Award for Poetry; Freddy Frankel (*In a Stone's Hollow*), recipient of the New England Writers Robert Penn Warren First Award in 2003; and Dorinda Clifton (*Woman in the Water: A Memoir of Growing Up in Hollywoodland*), featured at the 2006 Memphis Film Festival and recipient of a fellowship to the MacDowell Colony.

It is our hope that all our books express a commitment to quality in writing and publishing. Please visit www.bedbugpress.com for more information about the press.

COLOPHON

Titles are set in Trajan.
Text is set in Minion.

Typeset by ImPrint Services,
Corvallis, Oregon.